Visit to the dentist

Monica Hughes

www.heinemann.co.uk/library
Visit our website to find out more information about **Heinemann Library** books.

To order:
☎ Phone 44 (0) 1865 888066
▤ Send a fax to 44 (0) 1865 314091
▢ Visit the Heinemann Bookshop at www.heinemann.co.uk/library to browse our
   catalogue and order online.

First published in Great Britain by Heinemann
Library, Halley Court, Jordan Hill, Oxford
OX2 8EJ, part of Harcourt Education.
Heinemann is a registered trademark of Harcourt
Education Ltd.

Editorial: Sarah Eason and Georga Godwin
Design: Jo Hinton-Malivoire and Tokay,
Bicester, UK (www.tokay.co.uk)
Picture Research: Rosie Garai and Sally Smith
Production: Séverine Ribierre and Alex Lazarus

Originated by Dot Gradations Ltd
Printed and bound in China by South China
Printing Company

ISBN 0 431 18622 7 (hardback)
07 06 05 04 03
10 9 8 7 6 5 4 3 2 1

ISBN 0 431 18627 8 (paperback)
08 07 06 05 04
10 9 8 7 6 5 4 3 2 1

British Library Cataloguing in Publication Data
Hughes, Monica
Visit to the Dentist – My First
617.6
A full catalogue record for this book is available
from the British Library.

Acknowledgements
The Publishers would like to thank the following
for permission to reproduce photographs:
Gareth Boden **pp. 4**, **5**, **6**, **8**, **9**, **10**, **11**, **12**, **13**,
14, **15**, **16**, **17**, **18**, **20**, **21**, **22**, **23**; Rob Judges
p. 7; Science Photo Library/Alex Bartel **p. 19**.

Cover photograph is reproduced with permission
of Gareth Boden.

The Publishers would like to thank Philip Emmett
for his assistance in the preparation of this book.
We would also like to thank Dr Pradeep Bagga
and his staff.

Every effort has been made to contact copyright
holders of any material reproduced in this book.
Any omissions will be rectified in subsequent
printings if notice is given to the Publishers.

Contents

Going to the dentist

Remember to give your teeth a good clean before your visit.

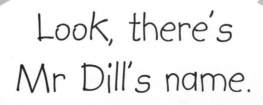

Look, there's
Mr Dill's name.

In the waiting room

What time is your appointment?

Tick, tock!
Tick, tock!

There are lots of fun things to do while we wait.

Meeting the dentist

What do you think of my chair?

The light can go up and down and forward and backward.

The dentist gets ready

There are lots of things to look at in the surgery.

The check-up

'All OK!', he says. The nurse writes up my notes.

13

Clean and polish

This is going to make my teeth really clean.

Bzzzzzzzzzzzz!
It feels nice and tickly!

14

Now I know how to clean my teeth properly.

17

Problem teeth
Have you got any fillings?

The brace makes
teeth straight.

Well done!

I'd like this sticker, please.

Can I have this toothbrush, Mum?

The next appointment

I mustn't forget to clean my teeth when I've finished.

Index

The end

Notes for adults

This series supports the child's knowledge and understanding of their world, in particular their personal, social and emotional development. The following Early Learning Goals are relevant to the series:

- respond to significant experiences, showing a range of feelings where appropriate
- develop an awareness of their own needs, views and feelings and be sensitive to the needs and feelings of others
- develop a respect for their own cultures and beliefs and those of other people
- manage their own personal hygiene
- introduce language that enables them to talk about their experiences in greater depth and detail.

Each book explores a range of different experiences, many of which will be familiar to the child. It is important that the child has the opportunity to relate the content of the book to their own experiences. This will be helped by asking the child open-ended questions, using phrases like: How would you feel? What do you think? What would you do? Time can be made to give the child the chance to talk about their worries or anxieties related to the new experiences.

Talking about the dentist
A visit to the dentist can seem less daunting if the young child has had the chance to watch a parent's teeth being examined beforehand. Parents can emphasize the fun of 'riding' in the dentist's chair, the tickling sensation in the mouth, spitting out and the sticker at the end! For those children who do have fillings the emphasis can be placed on the need to brush teeth regularly and avoid too many sweet foods and drinks.

Further activities
Follow-up activities could involve making a chart that can be ticked when the child has cleaned his/her teeth every morning and evening, perhaps using a new toothbrush and different toothpaste. It can also be fun to find which toys have teeth and to give each toy a 'check-up'.